TO:

FROM:

MW01104197

theCoupon Collection™

SOURCEBOOKS, INC.
NAPERVILLE, ILLINOIS

# The Perfect
# LIBRA
## Coupons

A coupon gift to inspire
the best in you

SOURCEBOOKS, INC.
NAPERVILLE, ILLINOIS

Published by Sourcebooks, Inc.
P.O. Box 4410, Naperville, Illinois 60567-4410
(630) 961-3900
FAX: (630) 961-2168
www.sourcebooks.com

ISBN 1-4022-0188-5

Printed and bound in the United States of America

AP 10 9 8 7 6 5 4 3 2 1

# THE PERFECT LIBRA
## *Born September 23 – October 22*

Welcome to the world of the perfect Libra. Astrology is a powerful symbolic language for describing and interpreting human life and events on the Earth. This coupon book is a fun way to dip into that ancient pool of knowledge and make the most of the potential that lies in your nature.

## WHY ASTROLOGY?

Astrologers believe that the makeup, configuration, and movement of the planets and stars correspond with events anywhere in the universe, including human lives, and that studying these cycles can help people understand the past and present, and even predict the future. By mapping the position of the other planets in our galaxy, the moon, and the sun in the heavens when you were born, astrology finds indications of the circumstances you may encounter, as well as clues to your basic personality traits and how you relate to others.

## THE TWELVE HOUSES

Imagine a wheel in space that circles the Earth like a cigar band. This band is divided into twelve sections, or houses, because the sun spends approximately one month in each area in relationship to the Earth, as our planet makes its yearly journey around the sun. (In ancient times, of course, it was believed that the sun was, in fact, circling the Earth.) The wheel of the Zodiac divides the heavens into the twelve traditional astrological groupings, each of which is assigned certain polarities, qualities, and elements. The Zodiac wheel also makes clear the relationships among the signs. For instance, Libra is located on the wheel directly opposite the sign of Aries, and is in many ways the Ram's opposite in values and interests.

Although the location of the sun at the time of your birth—your sun sign—provides the basic key to your personality, in astrology, *each* of the planets in our galaxy, as well as the moon, has influences which are expressed in your life.

## THE TWO POLARITIES

All the signs are divided into two polarities, either masculine or feminine types. The male signs are more active and extroverted, as in the Chinese philosophical term yang, which refers to the positive, bright, and masculine. The female signs are considered more sensitive, meditative, and inward looking, as in the Chinese yin, which is the negative, dark, and feminine. Of course, astrology has always acknowledged that everyone embodies both female and male energies in their nature.

As a Libra, your essence is masculine. You have strong male traits in your essential nature, which will interact with all the cultural and societal influences you encounter, as well as the other influences in your astrological chart (for instance, the location of the moon at your birth).

## THE THREE QUALITIES

A lesser known aspect of astrology divides the signs into three types of qualities—cardinal, fixed, or mutable—which have to do with how you relate to the world. The four mutable signs (Gemini, Virgo, Sagittarius, and Pisces) are the most changeable and open to outside influences.

The four fixed signs (Taurus, Leo, Scorpio, and Aquarius) are the most stable and the least concerned with outside influences—in fact, they tend to resist them.

As a Libra, you are one of the four cardinal signs, along with Aries, Cancer, and Capricorn. These signs are the most assertive, the most interested in making changes and being in control. The good news is, you can be a strong leader and a positive influence, all the while staying one step ahead of everyone else. The bad news is, you may tend to be controlling to the point of exploitation.

# THE FOUR ELEMENTS

Each sign of the Zodiac is also associated with one of the four elements: fire, earth, air, or water, which lend certain characteristics to those signs. The three fire signs are Aries, Leo, and Sagittarius—they tend to be energetic, impatient, explosive, and...well, fiery.

The three earth signs are Taurus, Virgo, and Capricorn. These earthy types are—you guessed it—down to earth. They tend to be practical, reliable, and cautious.

The emotional water signs are Cancer, Scorpio, and Pisces. These are the sensitive ones, the dreamers, the spiritualists. They are capable of great depths of emotion and compassion.

Libra is symbolized by the sign of the Scales. You, Libra, are one of the air signs of the Zodiac, along with Gemini and Aquarius. The Air signs are the thinkers, the intellectuals, and the planners. You are all about ideas, thought, and communication. Libra, in particular, has an airy quality that allows you to communicate with ease and social grace.

# THE FOUR ELEMENTS

Each sign of the Zodiac is also associated with one of the four elements: fire, earth, air, or water, which lend certain characteristics to those signs. The three fire signs are Aries, Leo, and Sagittarius—they tend to be energetic, impatient, explosive, and...well, fiery.

The three earth signs are Taurus, Virgo, and Capricorn. These earthy types are—you guessed it—down to earth. They tend to be practical, reliable, and cautious.

The emotional water signs are Cancer, Scorpio, and Pisces. These are the sensitive ones, the dreamers, the spiritualists. They are capable of great depths of emotion and compassion.

Libra is symbolized by the sign of the Scales. You, Libra, are one of the air signs of the Zodiac, along with Gemini and Aquarius. The Air signs are the thinkers, the intellectuals, and the planners. You are all about ideas, thought, and communication. Libra, in particular, has an airy quality that allows you to communicate with ease and social grace.

## YOUR RULING PLANETS

According to ancient astrology, the sun and moon ruled one house each, and the five other known planets (Mercury, Venus, Mars, Jupiter, and Saturn) ruled two houses each. As they were discovered, the farther distant planets of Uranus, Neptune, and Pluto were added to the ancient system, resulting in some houses having a "secondary" ruler.

You, Libra, are ruled by the planet Venus—the goddess of love. One of your major priorities is to establish balanced and harmonious relationships. You hesitate to display qualities you may consider counter to this end, such as anger. Venus rules all that is pleasant, graceful, and attractive. You may be drawn to express yourself as an artist—or you may find yourself in the pursuit of pleasure.

Libra is a masculine—positive, outgoing—sign, and you are both gregarious and much concerned with resolving conflicts. Remember that Venus also traditionally rules victory in war.

As a Libra, you are best understood through your symbol of the Scales. You are always weighing the possibilities, and sometimes find it difficult to make choices in your pursuit of peace and harmony.

## MIXING WITH THE OTHER ELEMENTS

As an Air sign, you can rely on the support of the Earth signs (Taurus, Virgo, and Capricorn) to keep you grounded. These friends will appreciate your calm, peaceful ways, and can help you make practical decisions when your tendency towards indecision is troubling you.

You have an affectionate nature that your Fire sign friends (Aries, Leo, and Sagittarius) will appreciate. Their energy can motivate you to choose from among the many possibilities you are always seeing, and act on it in a positive way.

The combination of Air and Water yields some beautiful possibilities. Around people of the Water signs (Cancer, Scorpio, and Pisces), Librans can express the poetry and beauty in their natures. The dreamy imaginations and sensitivity of the Water signs can elevate your intelligence and creativity to new heights. Just keep some Fire and Earth signs around to help keep you on track.

## WHAT'S YOUR MOON?

The position of the moon at your birth exerts a strong influence on the basic elements of your Libran personality. The house occupied by the Moon channels the expression of your personality in such areas as maternal qualities, domestic interests, and emotional needs.

For example, a moon in Aries brings fire and purpose to your easygoing Libran nature: as a parent, your Libran fairness and good communication skills will be complemented by Arien enthusiasm and warmth, making you an understanding and successful parent. In love, a moon in Aries brings additional passion to your generous Libran nature. You may want to investigate how your sun sign is tempered by the other influences in your astrological chart—it's both entertaining and a rich source of imagery and meaning.

# LIBRA IN LOVE

In general, Libras tend to be romantic and charming, but can also be flirtatious and changeable in their personal relationships. You are eager to establish intimacy with other people. Your agreeable nature and easy warmth make you a pleasant companion, although your indecisiveness can drive your partner crazy. At your best, you are loving, attractive, intelligent, and gentle. You might want to watch out for people who bring out your possible tendencies to be gullible and easily influenced, or lazy and self-indulgent.

Take a look at the coupons in this book: they are designed to help you explore your compatibility with other signs, bring out your best traits, and help you with your worst. Have a great time exploring the wisdom of the stars!

theCouponCollection™

SOURCEBOOKS, INC.®
NAPERVILLE, ILLINOIS

Since Libras need to keep life in balance,
now's the time to think about your next **VACATION**,
or a **CELEBRATION** of some kind.
Go ahead and make it elaborate.

Since they love to plan and adore travel, a Gemini would make the perfect partner for Libra when vacation planning.

To help your Libra **AIRINESS**
get a little grounded, try making something
out of clay or go and paint pottery.
You'll find this a soothing way
to express your creativity.

An earthy Virgo, who likes order, will be appreciated by the Libra who likes to keep all aspects of life harmonious.

Your element is air—
you'll never **FEEL SO FREE** as when
you're walking outside on a windy day.
With this coupon, take some time off
and go get in your element.

A Libra who hooks up
with a Gemini,
another Air sign, will
find a companion
who shares their love
of freedom.

Libra can be **SUPPORTED**
by coming into contact with the fire element.
On the next warm day, lie down in the
sun and soak up a few rays.

A fiery, energetic Aries and an affectionate Libra together make for a red-hot romance.

theCouponCollection™

SOURCEBOOKS, INC.
NAPERVILLE, ILLINOIS

Bring a little fire
into your airy EXISTENCE—
try wearing red, yellow, and orange.

The strong, warm-hearted Fire sign Leo with the sunny disposition provides perfect balance for the charming Libra.

theCouponCollection™

SOURCEBOOKS, INC.
NAPERVILLE, ILLINOIS

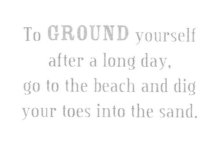

To **GROUND** yourself
after a long day,
go to the beach and dig
your toes into the sand.

The natural common sense and down-to-earth quality of a Virgo will be greatly appreciated by Libra.

the**Coupon**Collection™

SOURCEBOOKS, INC.™
NAPERVILLE, ILLINOIS

You're **EXPRESSIVE** and **COMMUNICATIVE**—
why not express yourself by singing at the top of your lungs?
This coupon entitles you to belt out one song of your choice—
either with the radio, alone in the shower,
or in front of friends.

When a happy-go-lucky Sagittarius teams up with an airy Libra, the results can be astonishing!

Are you being overly controlling in some area of your life?
Try a **RELEASING** yoga posture like "camel."
Sit up on your knees and bring your hands to the small of
your back. Stretch the front of your body and arch your
back. Breathe deeply until you feel you can release your
attachment to having things go all your way.

A sensitive, compassionate Cancer can provide Libra with the harmonious home life they seek.

the**Coupon**Collection™

SOURCEBOOKS, INC.®
NAPERVILLE, ILLINOIS

**EXPRESS** your Libra spirit—
wear a diaphanous scarf or shawl.

The esoteric, dreamy Pisces paired with the gregarious Libra will find no end of imaginative, creative fun.

the**Coupon**Collection™

Libra is a **SENSITIVE** and **THOUGHTFUL** leader. Today's the day to get that new idea of yours implemented. Grab a couple of cronies at work and get the ball rolling.

Hard-working, meticulous Virgo is the one that Libra needs to help give those brilliant ideas some solid reality.

the**Coupon**Collection™

SOURCEBOOKS, INC.®
NAPERVILLE, ILLINOIS

For a few minutes of Libra **PEACE**,
lie on the ground and gaze up at the clouds.

When a high-flying
Aquarius and a
knowledgeable Libra
get together, there's
no end to the flow of
ideas and creativity.

Libra is usually **POSITIVE** and **BRIGHT** no matter what happens. The next time something gets you down, use this coupon to do something really fun to cheer yourself up.

Libra, find yourself
an optimistic,
freedom-loving
Sagittarius, and you'll
never stop having
fun.

theCouponCollection™

SOURCEBOOKS, INC.
NAPERVILLE, ILLINOIS

It will always make a Libra **HAPPY** to hear the wind in the trees. Put up a wind chime and enjoy the beautiful sounds on a windy day.

A friendly Libra can help an intense, introverted Scorpio to open up, while the Scorpio's dark sensuality can bring emotional depth to the life of the intellectual Libra.

the Coupon Collection™

SOURCEBOOKS, INC.®
NAPERVILLE, ILLINOIS

**BLUE SAPPHIRE** is a Libra gem;
buy yourself a new piece of jewelry
or clothing in this color today.

Signs of the Zodiac
have long been
associated with
certain gems, metals,
animals, flowers, and
even herbs and
spices.

theCouponCollection™

SOURCEBOOKS, INC.
NAPERVILLE, ILLINOIS

Take care of your vulnerable Libran lower back—
treat yourself to a **SOOTHING MASSAGE**.

Each Zodiac sign is said to rule a particular part of the body—Libra rules the lumbar region and kidneys.

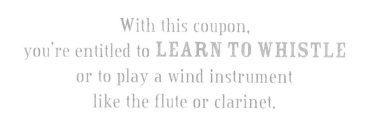

With this coupon,
you're entitled to **LEARN TO WHISTLE**
or to play a wind instrument
like the flute or clarinet.

Libra loves harmony of all kinds, and Gemini often enjoys playing music—they can make beautiful music together!

With this coupon,
**INDULGE YOURSELF**
on a hot-air balloon ride.
You'll be right in your element!

An adventurous,
passionate Aries
would love to sail off
into the wild blue
yonder with an airy
Libra.

theCouponCollection

SOURCEBOOKS, INC.
NAPERVILLE, ILLINOIS

The next time you find yourself unable
to make a choice between two options,
this coupon entitles you to do some
**LONG, DEEP YOGA BREATHING**.
Lie down on your back on the floor,
put your hand over your belly, and feel it
rise and fall as you inhale deeply and exhale slowly.

Libra and the serious
Capricorn will
complement each
other perfectly.

Flaunt that gregarious Libra personality—
**GO OUT DANCING.**

When an outgoing
Gemini teams up with
a sociable Sagittarius,
chances are good
you'll enjoy the
company of lots of
friends.

theCouponCollection™

SOURCEBOOKS, INC.
NAPERVILLE, ILLINOIS

## JUMP ON A TRAMPOLINE—
it's the closest you can get to flying!

Find a free-spirited
Gemini for a
playmate. They are
full of surprises,
making them lots of
fun to be around.

All those choices to make
can stop a Libra in your tracks.
Try a **LONG HOT BATH**—
the water element will calm you
down and make things clearer.

A Water sign like the
reserved but
passionate Scorpio
can be just what
Libras need to
balance their energy.

Libra is the communicator—
take this opportunity to
**SEND A LETTER**
or email to someone you
haven't seen in a long time.

Libra is exceptionally good at expressing thanks—just make sure you don't resent others for not thanking *you* profusely enough.

theCouponCollection™

SOURCEBOOKS, INC.
NAPERVILLE, ILLINOIS

You're **OUTGOING AND FRIENDLY**—
go out and meet someone new today.

Is there an Aquarius
in your future?
Aquarius and Libra
make ideal mates,
sharing a love for
beauty, society, and
art.

theCouponCollection™

SOURCEBOOKS, INC
NAPERVILLE ILLINOIS

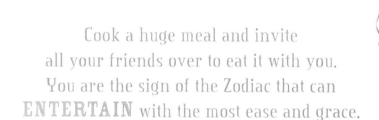

Cook a huge meal and invite
all your friends over to eat it with you.
You are the sign of the Zodiac that can
ENTERTAIN with the most ease and grace.

A loving Taurus can
provide the security
and sensuous comfort
that Libra will adore.

theCouponCollection™

SOURCEBOOKS, INC.®
NAPERVILLE, ILLINOIS

When you're feeling really undecided,
**GROUND** yourself by dressing in earth tones—
dark green, warm brown, golden yellow.

The company of a Capricorn can help keep Libra firmly rooted in the earth and provide balance.

theCouponCollection™

SOURCEBOOKS, INC.
NAPERVILLE, ILLINOIS

Your **ADAPTABLE NATURE** makes
you comfortable in many environments—today, just sit
down in the middle of your living room and
enjoy the comfort of your own home.

A gentle Virgo will be
sure to keep the
Libra's home
environment in
perfect order.

theCouponCollection™

SOURCEBOOKS, INC.
NAPERVILLE, ILLINOIS

**EARTHY ACTIVITIES** counterbalance feelings of insecurity. Pick up some acrylic paints and paint a rock for a doorstop.

A reliable, comfort-
loving Taurus is the
perfect companion for
a Libra who's looking
for a little security.

theCouponCollection™

SOURCEBOOKS, INC.®
NAPERVILLE, ILLINOIS

The next time it rains,
bring the water and earth elements
together to **GROUND** you—take off your shoes
and walk barefoot in a mud puddle.

Air signs like Libra
rely on Earth signs
for practical support
and Water signs for
emotional support.

theCouponCollection™

SOURCEBOOKS, INC.
NAPERVILLE, ILLINOIS

Bringing fire into your environment can make you feel **ENERGETIC** and **MOTIVATED**. Tonight, eat dinner by candlelight. If you want to go all out, light the whole house with candles.

Libra will adore the
company of the
golden Leo with the
radiant personality.

theCouponCollection™

SOURCEBOOKS, INC.™
NAPERVILLE, ILLINOIS

This coupon entitles you to **RELAX** after
a stressful day. Re-pot some houseplants,
or weed your garden. These activities
will soothe your busy mind.

A warm and sensual
Taurus will tend to
keep an indecisive
Libra in balance.

Use your **OUTGOING NATURE** to make other people feel more comfortable. Today go and welcome a new neighbor or co-worker. With you as the instigator, the conversation will be lively.

A Libra can look to the company of the quick-thinking Gemini for stimulating conversation.

Sometimes you make so many plans
that there isn't time for everything.
This coupon entitles you to
pare down your To Do list
to only a few items today. **DELEGATE**
or **FORGET** about the rest.

A powerful Leo can teach Libra a great deal about tactful delegation and skillful organization.

theCouponCollection™

SOURCEBOOKS, INC.®
NAPERVILLE, ILLINOIS

To get you centered, do some sit ups.
**REMEMBER TO BREATHE!**

A fellow Libra can
help you find all the
balance and harmony
you need in your life.

theCouponCollection™

SOURCEBOOKS, INC.®
NAPERVILLE, ILLINOIS

Libra always likes to be outside.
On the **NEXT WARM EVENING**,
take a picnic to the park.

That kind, sensitive Cancer would love to share a meal with a fascinating Libra, and Cancer is the best cook in the Zodiac!

theCouponCollection™

SOURCEBOOKS, INC.®
NAPERVILLE, ILLINOIS

When it's too hot to think,
use water to bring you back into **FOCUS**.
Run through a sprinkler or
take a dip in a lake or pool.

Libra will find the
company of a quirky
Pisces very
refreshing.

By nature Libra seeks
**BALANCE** and **HARMONY**.
The next time you feel out of balance,
take five deep breaths, then go back
to what you were doing.

Look to a charming
Taurus when you
want some peace and
comfort.

Libra is **ASSERTIVE** and a **STRONG LEADER**.
Now is the time to take stock of where you are and
where you're going. This coupon entitles you
to a quiet day completing half-finished projects
and making plans for new ones.

The intense Scorpio is brilliant at pursuing a goal with almost obsessive tenacity—a quality Libra could learn from.

theCouponCollection™

SOURCEBOOKS, INC.
NAPERVILLE, ILLINOIS

Libra is pleasant, graceful, and attractive.
This coupon entitles you to go out and have a
**WONDERFUL EVENING** with
your very best friends.

There's no better
company for a Libra
than another Libra—
you know what you
need without having
to ask.

theCouponCollection

SOURCEBOOKS, INC.
NAPERVILLE, ILLINOIS